3/15

United States Regions

Southwestern
Region

L.L. Owens

Rourke
Educational Media
rourkeeducationalmedia.com

Building Academic Vocabulary and Background Knowledge

Before reading a book, it is important to tap into what your child or students already know about the topic. This will help them develop their vocabulary, increase their reading comprehension, and make connections across the curriculum.

1. Look at the cover of the book. What will this book be about?
2. What do you already know about the topic?
3. Let's study the Table of Contents. What will you learn about in the book's chapters?
4. What would you like to learn about this topic? Do you think you might learn about it from this book? Why or why not?
5. Use a reading journal to write about your knowledge of this topic. Record what you already know about the topic and what you hope to learn about the topic.
6. Read the book.
7. In your reading journal, record what you learned about the topic and your response to the book.
8. After reading the book complete the activities below.

Content Area Vocabulary
Read the list. What do these words mean?

adobe

agriculture

arts

climate

culture

desert

geography

industry

irrigation

region

settlers

tourism

After Reading:

Comprehension and Extension Activity

After reading the book, work on the following questions with your child or students in order to check their level of reading comprehension and content mastery.

1. How did the Pueblo tribe shape the Southwestern region of the United States? (Summarize)
2. Describe the process of irrigation. (Summarize)
3. Would you like to live in the desert region? Why or why not? (Text to self connection)
4. How does adobe make living in the desert bearable? (Summarize)
5. Why did early Pueblo homes have doors on the second floor? (Asking questions)

Extension Activity

You make your own dam! You will need a plastic container, sand, water, rocks, and other materials such as sticks, wooden craft sticks, or tongue depressors. Pour a deep layer of sand in the large plastic container and carve out your river. Then build a dam in the middle of your river. Your dam needs to be strong and allow some water to flow through slowly. Once you've constructed your dam, pour water in your river. How did your design do? What changes could you make to construct a stronger dam? What were some obstacles?

Table of Contents

Introducing the Southwest

Certain images probably come to mind when you think of a specific United States area, or **region**. For the Southwest, you might think of:

- Hot, dry weather.
- A **desert** landscape dotted with cacti.
- Mountains and canyons.
- Foods like tamales and salsa.
- **Arts** and crafts like pottery and baskets.
- Animals like coyotes and rattlesnakes.

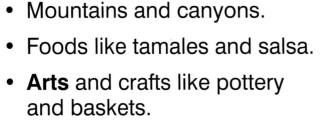

Geography is one of the oldest sciences. It's the study of Earth's physical features: land, air, water, and life forms.

That you get a mental picture of these things makes sense. All parts of a region must fit together somehow. When you study a region's **geography**, its special features tell a story. They offer clues about why people came to live there. You can see how the geography helped shape their way of life.

As the name suggests, the Southwest region is found in the southwestern part of the country. North of the Southwest is the Mountain region. To the south is Mexico. The southwestern landscape includes everything from majestic mountains to lush forests to wide-open deserts.

The Four Corners Monument marks the only spot in the nation where four states meet. This point is shared by Arizona, New Mexico, Colorado, and Utah.

This U.S. map outlines the Southwest region. Arizona and New Mexico make up a large portion of it. Other states with sections in the region are Texas, California, Nevada, Utah, and Colorado.

A Brief History

The Pueblo people were the first people to live in the Southwest. They were skilled farmers. They dug canals to help bring water to their crops. They grew corn, squash, and beans. They also grew cotton, peppers, and wheat. And they raised sheep and goats. Sometimes they hunted turkeys and rabbits.

The **climate** was very hot. The men farmed in the early morning or late in the day. During the hottest hours, they would stay busy indoors weaving clothes and blankets.

The Spanish word for town is pueblo. In the Southwest, a pueblo is a community of Native Americans. Today, the term Pueblo Indians refers to all Southwestern Native American tribes.

Navajo Churro Sheep

The Pueblo people celebrated the harvest with drum circles and dances.

Women also worked hard from sunrise to sunset. They raised children and kept the family home. They prepared all the food, spending part of every day grinding corn into flour.

Pueblo homes had flat roofs made of **adobe**, stone, and wood. The clay used in adobe helped keep the inside cool during hot days. On cold nights it released the heat it had absorbed. Southwestern pottery is made from similar clay.

Pueblo Home

Southwestern Pottery

Some early Pueblo homes were built on the sides of cliffs. Outside doors would be on the second floor, or higher. People entered using ladders hung from doorways. If they spotted enemies, they would pull up their ladders so attackers couldn't get in.

Spanish explorers came to the Southwest in the 1500s. They brought horses and new crops. They weren't there to help the native peoples. Their mission was to claim the land for themselves.

By the 1800s, Mexico had taken over much of the Southwest. American **settlers** felt the land belonged to them. Eventually, the two countries fought for ownership.

When the Mexican-American War (1846–1848) ended, Mexico signed over the land to the United States.

The Fall of the Alamo, 1836

When the dust cleared, Mexico had lost about one-third of its territory, including nearly all of present-day California, Utah, Nevada, Arizona, and New Mexico.

The Southwest would grow to become a vital and unique part of the United States.

Major Cities in the Modern Southwest		
Photo	City	Population
	Phoenix, Arizona	1.4 million
	El Paso, Texas	649,000
	Las Vegas, Nevada	584,000
	Albuquerque, New Mexico	546,000
	Tucson, Arizona	520,000

Big Industry

You can tell a lot about a region's unique features by the businesses, or industries, that succeed in it. **Industry** refers to a place's business activity as a whole. Important Southwest industries are **agriculture** and **tourism**.

Agriculture is big business in the Southwest. Ranchers raising cattle and sheep use much of the land. Farmers grow a variety of crops. The main ones are cotton, alfalfa, citrus, grains, hay, and sorghum. Other crops found in the region include onions, pecans, and potatoes.

Cotton Farm

Cooper Mine

Arizona has led copper production in the U.S. since 1910 and still enjoys that distinction, producing approximately 64 percent of domestic copper.

Most of the available fresh water is used for crops. Because the weather is so dry, extra water must be brought into the Southwest. The Colorado River and the Rio Grande are good sources. The Hoover Dam also stores water used for **irrigation.**

The Hoover Dam is on the Colorado River between Nevada and Arizona. Its functions are controlling flooding, generating electricity, and storing water for industrial use.

The Hoover Dam

Originally named the Boulder Dam, construction finished in 1936. The task took six years. It employed 21,000 workers and used 5 million barrels of concrete. The dam was renamed in 1947 for Herbert Hoover, America's 31st president. He was one of the project's biggest supporters.

The Southwest has a strong tourism industry. The dry, sunny climate attracts vacationers and retirees. The area boasts a seemingly endless supply of beautiful sights and fun activities.

People from all over the world visit Arizona to see the Grand Canyon. The Grand Canyon is the Southwest's most popular attraction. It's one of the Seven Natural Wonders of the World. Around 5 million tourists visit the Grand Canyon each year.

The city of Tombstone offers a glimpse of what life was like in the Old West. Popular tourist spots in New Mexico include Carlsbad Caverns and the International UFO Museum at Roswell.

More to See and Do
- Southeast California: The Glamis Sand Dunes
- Southern Utah: Navajo Mountain hiking trails
- Las Vegas, Nevada: Family-friendly shows and outdoor activities

Tombstone, Arizona

This vast canyon formed over time. The Colorado River's rushing waters actually carved it into the surrounding rock! Scientists think the canyon is about 5 to 6 million years old.

Nearly five million people travel here each year; 90 percent first see the canyon from the South Rim with its dramatic views into the deep inner gorge of the Colorado River.

Regional Culture

Modern Southwest **culture** reflects the region's history.

Language

For centuries, only Pueblo languages were spoken in the region. Spanish was introduced even before English. Much of the region was once part of Mexico, and many Spanish speakers live in today's Southwest.

Place names can illustrate the influence of other languages. The city name El Paso means, "the passageway" in Spanish. And Tucson, Arizona, got its name from a Pueblo word meaning, "village of the dark spring at the foot of the mountains."

SPANISH-ENGLISH

HOLA - HELLO
GRACIAS - THANKS
POR FAVOR - PLEASE
DE NADA - YOU'RE WELCOME

Architecture

Southwestern architecture is simple in style, and makes use of regional materials. Structures are built to stand up to the unique climate. There are many light-colored stucco homes with tiled floors that help keep things cool.

These beautiful blankets, or mantas, are similar to the ones made and worn by the Pueblos.

The Arts

The early settlers' influence is evident in a variety of regional arts. Pottery, music, dance, jewelry, sculpture, and hand-woven fabrics all display an unmistakable Southwestern flare.

Food

Traditional Southwest cooking involves methods and ingredients easily traced to the many cultures that formed the region. A Mexican influence is seen in the use of corn, beans, chiles, and chocolate. The Spanish introduced meats like lamb, pork, and beef. Other settlers brought in wheat, tomatoes, melons, and peaches.

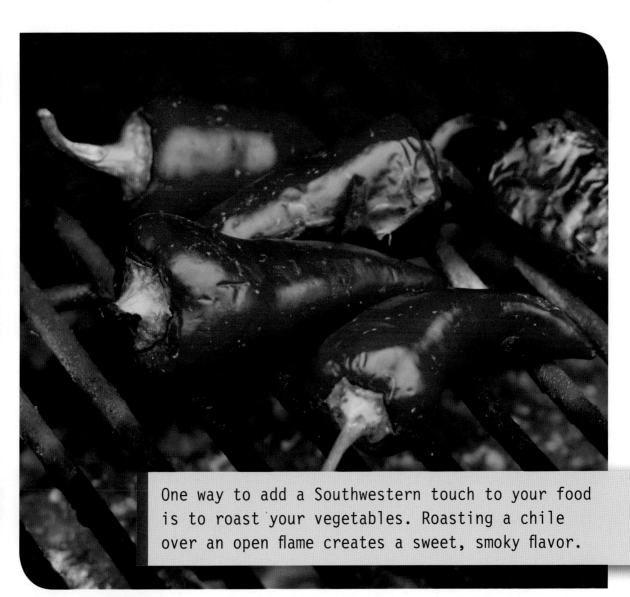

One way to add a Southwestern touch to your food is to roast your vegetables. Roasting a chile over an open flame creates a sweet, smoky flavor.

This snack layers several Southwestern flavors. The dip is easy to make, easy to pair with other foods, and easy to eat! Wherever you live, you can enjoy the flavor of the American Southwest.

Zippy Southwestern Dip

Ingredients:

$1\frac{1}{2}$ cups sour cream

$\frac{1}{2}$ cup mayonnaise

1 teaspoon ground cumin

$\frac{1}{2}$ teaspoon chili powder

$\frac{1}{4}$ teaspoon garlic salt

$\frac{1}{4}$ teaspoon onion powder

$\frac{1}{4}$ teaspoon paprika

$\frac{3}{4}$ cup shredded cheddar cheese

1 small can chopped green chiles, drained

Directions:

In a medium bowl, mix all ingredients from sour cream through paprika. Next, stir in the cheese and chiles. Cover and refrigerate for up to 4 hours. Serve with tortilla chips.

State Facts Sheet

Arizona

Motto: God Enriches.

Nickname: The Grand Canyon State;
  The Copper State

Capital: Phoenix

Known for: Desert Landscape,
  Saguaro Cactus, the Grand Canyon

Fun Fact: The bola tie is the official
  state neckware.

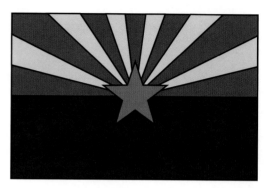

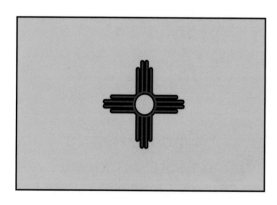

New Mexico

Motto: It Grows as it Goes.

Nickname: The Land of Enchantment

Capital: Santa Fe

Known for: Beautiful Scenery, Unique
  Cuisine, Uranium, Roswell

Fun Fact: The state's longest river, the
  Rio Grande, runs the entire length of
  New Mexico.

Texas

Motto: Friendship.

Nickname: The Lone Star State

Capital: Austin

Known for: Longhorn Cattle,
the Alamo, Cowboys, Oil, Barbeque

Fun Fact: Texas was an independent
nation from 1836 to 1845.

California

Motto: Eureka, I Have Found It.

Nickname: The Golden State

Capital: Sacramento

Known for: Hollywood, Beaches, Wine
Country, Golden Gate Bridge

Fun Fact: In California, Death Valley is
the hottest, driest place in the U.S. It
reaches 115° Fahrenheit (46° Celsius)
in summer.

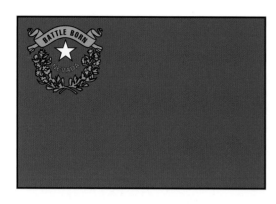

Nevada

Motto: All For Our Country.

Nickname: The Silver State

Capital: Carson City

Known for: Desert, Mountains, Mining, Gold, Las Vegas, Gambling

Fun Fact: Nevada is the largest gold-producing state in the nation.

Utah

Motto: Industry.

Nickname: The Beehive State

Capital: Salt Lake City

Known for: Rock Formations, the Great Salt Lake, Skiing

Fun Fact: Utah is named for the Ute tribe, which means people of the mountains.

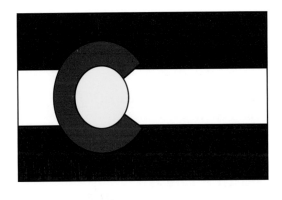

Colorado

Motto: Nothing Without Providence.

Nickname: The Centennial State

Capital: Denver

Known for: Skiing, Rocky Mountains, Pike's Peak, Forests, Mining

Fun Fact: The world's largest flattop mountain is in Grand Mesa.

Glossary

adobe (uh-DOH-bee): bricks made of clay and straw dried in the sun

agriculture (ARG-ri-kuhl-chur): the raising of crops and animals

arts (ahrts): making and sharing works of art

climate (KLYE-mit): the everyday weather of a place

culture (KUHL-chur): the way of life for a group of people

desert (DES-urt): dry land with little rainfall and few plants

geography (jee-AH-gruh-fee): the physical features of a place

industry (IN-duh-stree): businesses found in a community

irrigation (ir-uh-GAY-shuhn): system for supplying water to crops

region (REE-juhn): a specific geographic area

settlers (SET-lurz): people who create homes in a new place

tourism (toor-izm): visiting a place for pleasure

Index

Show What You Know

1. Which area of scientific study explores Earth's physical features?
2. Who were the first inhabitants of the Southwest?
3. When did the Mexican-American War end?
4. Why was the Hoover Dam built?
5. How was the Spanish language introduced to the Southwestern region?

Websites to Visit

www.nps.gov/grca/forkids/fact-sheets.htm

www.ducksters.com/history/native_americans/pueblo_tribe.php

www.britannica.com/EBchecked/topic/556966/Southwest

Author

Originally from the Midwest, L.L. Owens now lives in the Pacific Northwest. She has written more than 80 books for children and loves working with both nonfiction and fiction. Learn more about her at www.llowens.com.

Meet The Author!
www.meetREMauthors.com

www.rourkeeducationalmedia.com

PHOTO CREDITS: Cover: ©CarbonBrain (top left), ©Missing35mm (top middle), ©Loneburro (top right), ©Sara Winter (bottom left), ©Marcus Lindström (bottom right); title page: ©John Wollwerth; page 3: ©Elena Ray; page 4: ©Eric Isselee (left), ©SuziMcGregor (middle), ©Samuel Borges Photography (right); page 5: ©fotostorm; page6: ©spiritofamerica (top), ©Legacy Imges (bottom); page 7: ©lfreytag; page 8: ©MonaMakela; page 9: Courtesy of National Archives and Records Administration; page 10: ©Vladislav Gajic (top), ©jamirae (bottom); page 11: ©kingjon; page 12: Texas State Library & Archives Commsion; page 13: ©Marcus Lindström, ©Frontpage, ©littleny, ©gary yim, ©Todd Taulman (top to bottom); page14: ©Jim David; page 15: ©Tim Roberts Photography; page16-17: ©Matejh Photography; page 18: ©powerofforever; page 19: ©Sumikophoto; page 21: ©photoBeard; page22: ©Slattery & Crist Photography; page 23: ©akaplummer; page 25: ©Lisa Young; Pg 28, 29 © Turovsky

Edited by: Jill Sherman

Cover design by: Jen Thomas
Interior design by: Rhea Magaro

Library of Congress PCN Data

Southwestern Region / L.L. Owens
(United States Regions)
ISBN 978-1-62717-668-2 (hard cover)
ISBN 978-1-62717-790-0 (soft cover)
ISBN 978-1-62717-907-2 (e-Book)
Library of Congress Control Number: 2014934376
Printed in the United States of America, North Mankato, Minnesota

Also Available as:

ROURKE'S e-Books